I0409022

Top 10 marketing strategy

First published by Samir Saif 2023

First edition

Advisor: Growth mind academy

© Samir Saif

Marketing Strategy Definition

A marketing strategy is a plan for promoting and selling products or services. It involves analyzing the target market, identifying the right customers, and figuring out how to reach and persuade them effectively.

A marketing strategy should include a variety of tactics, such as advertising, social media, email campaigns, and events, and should be aligned with the overall business goals. To develop a marketing strategy, it can be helpful to conduct market research, define your brand, and set specific objectives.

Consider the following while establishing a marketing strategy:
Define your target audience: Who are you trying to reach with your marketing efforts?

Understanding your target audience will help you create messaging and content that resonates with them.

Determine your value proposition: What makes your product or service unique and valuable to your customers?

Your value proposition should be a key part of your marketing strategy.

Set specific, measurable, achievable, relevant, and time-bound (SMART) goals: Your marketing strategy should include specific goals that you want to achieve, such as increasing website traffic or generating leads. Make sure your goals are SMART, meaning they are specific, measurable, achievable, relevant, and time-bound.

Determine your budget: How much money do you have available for marketing? Your budget will help you determine which tactics and channels you can afford to use.

Choose marketing channels: There are many ways to reach potential customers, such as advertising, social media, content marketing, email marketing, and events. Consider which channels are most appropriate for your business and your target audience.

Create a content marketing plan: Content marketing is a key part of many marketing strategies. It involves creating valuable, relevant, and consistent content to attract and retain a clearly defined audience. Develop a plan for creating and promoting content that aligns with your business goals.

Monitor and analyze your results: It's important to track the success of your marketing efforts so you can determine what's working and what's not. Use tools like Google Analytics to monitor your website traffic and conversions, and use social media analytics to track the performance of your social media campaigns.

Test and optimize: Don't be afraid to try new things and see what works best for your business. Consider A/B testing different elements of your marketing campaigns, such as subject lines, call-to-action buttons, and ad copy, to see which versions perform the best.

Be consistent: Consistency is key to building trust and credibility with your audience. Make sure your branding and messaging is consistent across all marketing channels.

Stay up-to-date: The marketing landscape is constantly changing, so it's important to stay up-to-date on the latest trends and best practices. Consider joining industry groups and attending marketing conferences to stay informed.

Use customer insights: Make sure you have a deep understanding of your customers and their needs and preferences. Use tools like customer surveys and focus groups to gather customer insights, and use this information to inform your marketing decisions.

Build relationships: Marketing is not just about promoting your products or services, it's also about building relationships with your customers. Focus on providing value and creating a positive customer experience, and you'll be more likely to turn customers into loyal advocates for your business.

Integrate your marketing efforts: Your marketing strategy should be integrated across all channels and touch points. Make sure your messaging is consistent and that your marketing efforts work together to support your overall business goals.

Collaborate with other businesses: Consider partnering with complementary businesses to reach new audiences and cross-promote each other's products or services.

Be agile: Be flexible and willing to adjust your marketing strategy as needed. Don't be afraid to try new things and pivot if something isn't working.

Utilize social media: Social media can be a powerful marketing tool, especially for reaching younger consumers. Consider which social media platforms your target audience is most active on, and create a presence on those platforms.

Use email marketing: Email marketing can be an effective way to stay in touch with customers and promote your products or services. Consider building an email list and sending newsletters, promotional emails, or automated email campaigns.

Invest in search engine optimization (SEO): SEO involves optimizing your website and online content to rank higher in search engine results. This can help you attract more qualified traffic to your site and improve your visibility online.

Use influence marketing: Influence marketing involves partnering with influences in your industry or niche to promote your products or services. Influences have large followings and can help you reach a wider audience.

Consider paid advertising: Paid advertising, such as Google Ad Words or Facebook Ads, can be a effective way to reach specific target audiences. However, it's important to track the results of your paid advertising efforts and make sure you are getting a good return on investment.

Create a mobile-friendly website: With the increasing use of smartphones, it's important to make sure your website is mobile-friendly. A mobile-friendly website will provide a better user experience for mobile users and may also rank higher in mobile search results.

Use video marketing: Video can be a powerful marketing tool, as it's more engaging and easier to consume than text. Consider creating videos to promote your products or services, or to share educational or entertaining content with your audience.

Utilize user-generated content: User-generated content, such as reviews or social media posts, can be a powerful marketing tool. Encourage your customers to share their experiences with your products or services, and consider featuring user-generated content on your website or social media accounts.

Consider implementing chat bots: Chat bots can be a useful way to provide customer service and support, as well as promote your products or services. Chat bots can be integrated into your website or social media accounts and can provide instant responses to customer inquiries.

Use re targeting ads: Re targeting ads are ads that are shown to users who have previously visited your website. These ads can be effective in reminding users about your products or services and encouraging them to make a purchase.

Utilize virtual and augmented reality: Virtual and augmented reality technologies can be used to create immersive marketing experiences. Consider using VR or AR to showcase your products or services in a unique and engaging way.

Use content personalization: Personalized content can be more effective at engaging customers and encouraging conversions. Consider using tools that allow you to personalize your website or emails based on user data, such as location or past purchases.

Utilize customer loyalty programs: Customer loyalty programs can be a useful way to reward and retain customers. Consider offering loyalty rewards, such as discounts or exclusive perks, to encourage repeat purchases.

Use referral marketing: Referral marketing involves encouraging satisfied customers to refer your products or services to their friends or colleagues. Consider implementing a referral program to encourage customers to spread the word about your business.

Utilize experiential marketing: Experiential marketing involves creating immersive, interactive experiences for customers. Consider hosting events or creating pop-up shops to give customers the opportunity to engage with your brand in a meaningful way.

1. Growth Hacking market strategy

Growth hacking is a concept that was popularized in the startup world, but it can be applied to businesses of any size. The key elements of growth hacking are a focus on growth, a data-driven approach, and a willingness to try unconventional methods. Growth hackers are constantly experimenting and testing different tactics to find the ones that work best for their business.

One of the key principles of growth hacking is to focus on the metrics that matter most to the business. This could be things like website traffic, user acquisition, or customer retention. Growth hackers track these metrics closely and use them to guide their efforts and measure the success of their tactics.

Growth hacking can be a powerful tool for businesses looking to accelerate their growth, but it's important to remember that it is not a substitute for traditional marketing. It is just one approach that can be used to drive growth, and it is most effective when it is part of a well-rounded marketing strategy.

Tactics that growth hackers might use to drive growth

There are many different tactics that growth hackers might use to drive growth. Some common techniques include:

Viral marketing: Creating content or campaigns that are designed to be shared widely through social media and other channels.

SEO: Optimizing a website to rank highly in search engine results for relevant keywords.

Content marketing: Creating and sharing valuable, relevant, and consistent content to attract and retain a clearly defined audience.

Email marketing: Using email to communicate with and nurture relationships with potential and existing customers.

Social media marketing: Using social media platforms to promote a business and its products or services.

Influencer marketing: Partnering with influences (people with a large social media following) to promote a product or service.

Growth hacking can be a very effective way to drive rapid growth, particularly in the early stages of a business. However, it is important to have a solid understanding of your target audience and to be willing to experiment and learn from your efforts. It is also important to remember that not all growth hacking tactics will work for every business, so it is important to be flexible and open to trying new things.

Here are a few more things to consider when it comes to growth hacking:

Collaboration: Growth hacking often requires collaboration across different departments, such as marketing, sales, and product development. It's important to bring a diverse set of perspectives to the table and to work together to find the best growth strategies for your business.

Data-driven decision making: Growth hacking is all about using data to guide your decision making. It's important to track key metrics and to use data to understand what's working and what isn't.

Continuous improvement: Growth hacking is an ongoing process, not a one-time event. It's important to continuously test and optimize your strategies to find the best ways to drive growth.

Scaling: Once you find a growth strategy that works, it's important to be able to scale it up to reach a larger audience. This may require adapting your approach or finding new channels to reach more people.

Examples of a growth marketing companies

Many companies use growth marketing to drive user acquisition, retention, and revenue growth. Some examples of companies that have used growth marketing effectively include:

1. Dropbox Growth Marketing Campaign:

Dropbox is a file hosting service that offers cloud storage, file synchronization, and client software. In its early days, Dropbox used a referral program as a key part of its growth marketing strategy. The company offered users additional storage space for every new user they invited to join Dropbox.

This helped the company grow from 100,000 users to 4 million users in just 15 months. This referral program was very successful and helped Dropbox grow rapidly.

Other growth marketing campaigns that Dropbox has used include partnerships with other companies, such as Samsung and Adobe, to offer Dropbox as a built-in feature on their devices and software.

Dropbox has also used content marketing and search engine optimization to increase its visibility online and attract new users.

Overall, Dropbox's growth marketing strategy has been focused on creating value for its users and finding ways to incentivize them to invite their friends and colleagues to join the service.

2. Airbnb Growth Marketing Campaign:

Airbnb is a great example of a company that has experienced significant growth through marketing campaigns. One key aspect of Airbnb's marketing strategy has been its focus on creating a strong brand identity and building a sense of community among its users.

This has involved creating engaging and visually appealing marketing materials, as well as developing partnerships and sponsorships with events and organizations that align with Airbnb's values.

Airbnb has also made use of social media and influencer marketing to reach a wider audience and create buzz around its brand. Additionally, Airbnb has implemented referral programs and other incentives to encourage its users to invite their friends and family to join the platform.

All of these efforts have contributed to Airbnb's rapid growth and its position as a major player in the online travel and accommodation industry.

Here are a few more details on Airbnb's marketing efforts:

Customer experience: Airbnb places a strong emphasis on the customer experience, and has worked to make the process of booking and staying in an Airbnb property as seamless and enjoyable as possible.

This has included the development of a user-friendly website and mobile app, as well as the introduction of features such as verified listings and a comprehensive host rating system. By focusing on the customer experience, Airbnb has been able to attract and retain a large user base.

Marketing partnerships: Airbnb has entered into a number of marketing partnerships with companies and organizations in various industries. For example, Airbnb has partnered with airlines, hotels, and event organizers to offer unique travel experiences and packages to its users. These partnerships help Airbnb to reach new audiences and strengthen its brand association with various types of travel.

Content marketing: Airbnb has also made use of content marketing to showcase the unique properties and experiences available on its platform, and to highlight the personal stories of its hosts and guests.

Airbnb has used a variety of formats for this content, including blog posts, social media posts, and videos, and has often featured user-generated content in its marketing efforts. This content has helped to create a strong emotional connection with Airbnb's audience and to build brand loyalty.

Public relations: Airbnb has also engaged in public relations efforts to build awareness and positive sentiment around its brand. This has included working with journalists and bloggers to secure coverage of Airbnb's products and services, as well as engaging with its users and responding to customer feedback on social media. By proactively managing its public image, Airbnb has been able to shape the way that it is perceived by the public and to mitigate any negative publicity.

Slack Growth Marketing Campaign:

Slack is a messaging and collaboration platform that has experienced rapid growth in recent years. Here is an example of how Slack could use growth marketing tactics to drive user acquisition and growth:

Offer a free trial: Slack offers a free trial of its paid plans, which allows users to try out the platform before committing to a paid subscription. This can be an effective way to convert free users into paying customers.

Utilize referrals: Slack has a referral program that rewards users for inviting their colleagues and friends to join the platform. This can be an effective way to drive word-of-mouth growth and bring in new users.

Use content marketing: Slack can create educational content, such as blog posts and videos, that demonstrate the value of the platform to potential users. This can be an effective way to attract and engage new users.

Utilize social media: Slack can use social media platforms, such as Twitter and Linked In, to reach new users and engage with its target audience.

Utilize search engine optimization (SEO): Slack can optimize its website and content to rank highly in search engine results, making it more visible to potential users who are searching for collaboration and messaging tools.

LinkedIn Growth Marketing Campaign:

LinkedIn is a professional networking platform that allows users to connect with other professionals, search for jobs, and join industry groups.

While LinkedIn can be a powerful tool for marketing and growing a business, it is not typically thought of as a platform for conducting growth marketing campaigns. Growth marketing campaigns are typically focused on testing and optimizing various marketing tactics in order to drive user acquisition, engagement, and retention.

These campaigns often involve using data and analytics to identify and target specific segments of users, and then using a variety of marketing channels (e.g. email, social media, content marketing) to reach and engage those users. LinkedIn can certainly be a useful channel for these campaigns, but it is not the primary focus.

Pinterest Growth Marketing Campaign:

Pinterest is a social media platform that allows users to discover and save ideas for their various interests, such as home decor, fashion, and cooking. It is a visual platform that allows users to create and share collections of images and videos, known as "pins," on virtual boards.

Pinterest has used a variety of growth marketing techniques to increase its user base and engagement. Some examples of these techniques include:

Referral marketing: Pinterest has a referral program that rewards users with additional features when they invite their friends to join the platform.

Content marketing: Pinterest has a large library of helpful articles and videos that provide users with ideas and inspiration for their various interests. This content is designed to engage users and keep them coming back to the platform.

Search engine optimization (SEO): Pinterest has optimized its site to rank well in search engine results, which makes it easier for users to discover the platform when searching for relevant keywords.

Social media marketing: Pinterest has a strong presence on social media platforms like Twitter, Facebook, and Instagram, which helps to attract new users to the platform.

Paid advertising: Pinterest has also used paid advertising campaigns to reach new users and increase engagement on the platform.

Overall, Pinterest's growth marketing efforts have been successful in attracting and retaining a large user base, which has helped the platform become a popular destination for discovering and sharing ideas.

There are several ways that businesses can use Pinterest for growth marketing:

- Create a Pinterest business account and optimize your profile with keywords related to your business.
- Use high-quality, visually appealing images and videos to showcase your products or services.
- Create boards related to your business and populate them with pins that link back to your website or blog.
- Use Pinterest's promoted pins feature to reach a larger audience and drive traffic to your website.
- Utilize Pinterest analytics to track the performance of your pins and boards and make adjustments to your strategy as needed.

By following these strategies, businesses can effectively use Pinterest as a growth marketing tool to attract and engage potential customers.

Growth Marketing Tool List:

There are many tools that can be helpful for growth marketing. Some popular options include:

- Google Analytics: This tool allows you to track and analyze website traffic, as well as understand the behavior of visitors on your site.
- Hotjar: This tool provides heatmaps and session recordings that can help you understand how visitors are interacting with your website.
- SEMrush: This is a tool for search engine optimization (SEO) and pay-per-click (PPC) advertising. It can help you improve your search engine rankings and run more effective PPC campaigns.
- Ahrefs: This is another SEO tool that can help you improve your search engine rankings and track the performance of your website.
- Mailchimp: This is an email marketing tool that can help you send newsletters and other email campaigns to your subscribers.

- Hootsuite: This is a social media management tool that can help you schedule and publish content, as well as track the performance of your social media accounts.
- Intercom: This is a customer communication platform that can help you communicate with your customers in real-time, through live chat, email, and messaging.
- Optimizely: This is a tool for A/B testing, which allows you to test different versions of your website or app to see which performs better.
- Google Ads: This is Google's advertising platform that allows you to run pay-per-click (PPC) campaigns on Google search and other sites across the internet.
- LinkedIn Ads: This is LinkedIn's advertising platform that allows you to run PPC campaigns on the LinkedIn network. It can be particularly useful for B2B companies looking to reach a professional audience.
- Crazy Egg: This tool provides heatmaps and other visualizations that can help you understand how visitors are interacting with your website.

- Airtable: This is a flexible and customizable database tool that can help you organize and track data related to your growth marketing efforts.
- HubSpot: This is a comprehensive marketing, sales, and customer service platform that includes a range of tools for growth marketing, including email marketing, social media management, and more.
- Segment: This is a customer data platform (CDP) that allows you to collect, manage, and segment your customer data from multiple sources.
- Appcues: This is a tool for creating in-app messages, walkthroughs, and other onboarding experiences to help users get the most out of your product.
- Amplitude: This is an analytics platform that helps you understand user behavior and track key metrics related to growth.

These are just a few examples, but there are many other growth marketing tools available as well. It's important to choose the tools that are most relevant to your needs and goals.

Overall, growth hacking is a powerful tool for businesses looking to accelerate their growth. By being data-driven, creative, and willing to try unconventional tactics, businesses can find new and effective ways to reach their target audience and drive growth.

Growth hacking can be a very effective way to drive rapid growth, but it's important to keep in mind that it is not a magic bullet. Here are a few things to keep in mind when it comes to growth hacking:

It requires a lot of experimentation: Growth hacking requires a lot of trial and error, and not all tactics will work for every business. It's important to be willing to experiment and to learn from your efforts.

It's not a substitute for a solid product: No amount of marketing or growth hacking can make up for a product or service that is not meeting the needs of your customers. It's important to have a solid product or service that meets the needs of your target market.

It's not a one-time effort: Growth hacking is an ongoing process, and it's important to continuously test and optimize your strategies to find the best ways to drive growth.

It's not a replacement for traditional marketing: While growth hacking can be a powerful tool for driving growth, it should not be seen as a replacement for traditional marketing. It's important to have a well-rounded marketing strategy that includes a mix of tactics, including both traditional and growth hacking approaches.

Overall, growth hacking can be a very effective way to drive rapid growth, particularly in the early stages of a business. However, it's important to approach it with a clear strategy and to be open to experimentation and learning from your efforts.

2. Guerrilla marketing Strategy

Guerrilla marketing is a marketing strategy in which a company uses unconventional and low-cost tactics to promote a product or service. The goal is to create a unique, engaging, and memorable experience for the consumer, often in a location where they are not expecting it. The term "guerrilla marketing" was coined by Jay Conrad Levinson in his 1984 book "Guerrilla Marketing."
Some examples of guerrilla marketing include street performances, viral campaigns, and scavenger hunts. These types of marketing efforts are designed to be unexpected and create a buzz around the product or service being promoted. The goal of guerrilla marketing is to create a high impact marketing campaign that is low cost and easy to execute. It relies on the element of surprise to capture the attention of the consumer and create a memorable experience.

Key Principles Guerrilla Marketing

The key principles of guerrilla marketing are:

- Be creative: Use your creativity to come up with unique marketing ideas that will grab the attention of your target audience.
- Be unexpected: Use unexpected marketing tactics and techniques to surprise and delight your audience.

- Be personal: Connect with your audience on a personal level by tailoring your marketing messages to their needs, interests, and values.
- Be timely: Time your marketing efforts to coincide with relevant events, holidays, or news stories to increase their impact.
- Be resourceful: Use whatever resources you have available to you to get your message out there, whether it's social media, your website, or even word of mouth.
- Be persistent: Keep trying new marketing techniques and ideas until you find what works for your business.
- Use humor: A touch of humor can go a long way in engaging your audience and making your marketing efforts more memorable.
- Utilize word of mouth: Encourage your customers to spread the word about your business through word-of-mouth marketing. This can be as simple as asking them to tell their friends and family about your products or services, or offering incentives for referrals.
- Leverage technology: Use technology to your advantage by incorporating it into your marketing efforts. For example, you can use social media, email marketing, or mobile marketing to reach your audience.
- Be authentic: Be genuine and authentic in your marketing efforts. Don't try to be something you're not, and be transparent about your products and services.
- Be bold: Don't be afraid to take risks with your marketing. Sometimes, the boldest and most unconventional approaches can be the most effective.
- Think locally: Consider the specific needs and interests of your local community and tailor your marketing efforts to them.

- Use storytelling: Use storytelling to engage your audience and make your marketing more compelling. Share the story of your business and how it came to be, or use storytelling to illustrate the benefits of your products or services.
- Be visual: Use visual elements like images, videos, and graphics to make your marketing more appealing and attention-grabbing.
- Be interactive: Encourage your audience to participate in your marketing efforts by creating interactive campaigns or contests.
- Be flexible: Be prepared to adapt and adjust your marketing efforts as needed. What works for one business may not work for another, so be open to trying new approaches and experimenting with different techniques.

Many different companies have used guerrilla marketing to promote their products or services. Here are a few examples:

Nike Guerrilla Marketing Campaign:

One example of a guerrilla marketing campaign by Nike was the "Nike Grind" campaign. This campaign involved Nike re purposing old athletic shoes, apparel, and equipment into new products, such as courts and playgrounds.
The goal of the campaign was to promote sustainability and reduce waste, while also raising awareness about Nike's commitment to the environment.
The campaign was implemented through a series of events, including the creation of pop-up Grind shops, where people could drop off their old Nike gear to be recycled, and the

installation of Grind-themed playgrounds and courts in cities around the world.

The campaign received widespread media coverage and helped to enhance Nike's reputation as a socially and environmentally responsible company.

Another example of a guerrilla marketing campaign by Nike was the "Human Chain" campaign, which was launched in 2011 to promote the brand's line of running shoes.

The campaign involved creating a chain of runners in various cities around the world, with each runner wearing a pair of Nike running shoes and holding hands with the person next to them.

The runners formed a chain that stretched for miles, passing through iconic landmarks and high-traffic areas.

The campaign was designed to create a sense of community and encourage people to take up running as a sport.

It was promoted through social media, with people invited to join the chain by posting pictures and videos of themselves running with the hashtag #Nike Human Chain.

The campaign was successful in generating buzz and getting people excited about running and Nike's running shoes.

Red Bull Guerrilla Marketing campaign:

Red Bull is known for its innovative and unconventional marketing campaigns. One example of a guerrilla marketing campaign by Red Bull is the "Red Bull Stratus" project, in which the company sponsored skydiver Felix Kindergartner's record-breaking jump from the edge of space in 2012.

The jump was watched by millions of people around the world, and the Red Bull brand received widespread media coverage and attention as a result. Red Bull also sponsors a number of extreme sports events and athletes, and uses these sponsorship as opportunities to promote its brand and products through creative marketing campaigns.In 2013, Red Bull created a "human-powered flight" campaign to promote its energy drink. The campaign featured a human-powered helicopter that was designed and built by a team of engineers and pilots.

The helicopter successfully flew for over a minute, setting a new world record. Red Bull promoted the campaign through social media, online videos, and other marketing materials. Red Bull has also sponsored a number of music festivals and events, such as the Red Bull Music Academy, a series of music workshops and events held in cities around the world. As part of these sponsorship, Red Bull often creates interactive installations and experiences for attendees, such as a "silent disco" where participants can listen to music through wireless headphones.

Red Bull has also been known to use ambient marketing techniques, such as placing branded stickers and posters in unexpected places around cities, or creating temporary art installations and murals in public spaces. These campaigns aim to catch people's attention and create a buzz around the brand. Overall, Red Bull's marketing campaigns are known for being creative, engaging, and memorable, and often involve a combination of traditional and non-traditional marketing tactics.

Starbucks Guerrilla Marketing Campaigns:

Starbucks has used several guerrilla marketing campaigns to promote its brand and products.

One example is the "Starbucks Melody" campaign, which involved placing music CDs in Starbucks stores that contained songs chosen by the company's employees.

Customers could listen to the CDs in the store or purchase them to take home. This campaign was designed to create a more enjoyable and personalized experience for Starbucks customers, while also promoting the company's music selection.

Another example of a guerrilla marketing campaign by Starbucks was the "Green Apron Delivery" campaign, which involved Starbucks employees wearing green aprons and delivering coffee and other products to customers in various locations around a city. The campaign was designed to create a sense of surprise and excitement among customers, while also promoting the company's delivery service.

Netflix Guerrilla Marketing campaign:

A guerrilla marketing campaign for Netflix might involve using social media to create buzz around a new show or movie, organizing events or contests to engage with viewers, or using street art or other visually striking elements to create a sense of mystery or excitement.

Here are a few more examples of guerrilla marketing campaigns that Netflix might use:

Partnering with local businesses to promote a new show or movie. For example, a coffee shop might offer a special drink inspired by a popular Netflix show, or a bookstore might create a window display featuring books that were adapted into movies or shows on Netflix.

Using social media to generate buzz and engage with viewers. This could involve creating social media posts that showcase behind-the-scenes footage, hosting Q&A sessions with actors or creators, or using hashtags to encourage viewers to share their own content related to a show or movie.

Creating immersive experiences or events that allow people to feel like they are part of the show or movie. For example, Netflix might create a pop-up shop or exhibit that allows people to explore the world of a particular show or movie, or host a screening event that includes interactive elements or special guests.

Using street art or other forms of public art to generate interest and create a sense of mystery. This could involve creating murals or other large-scale artworks that are related to a show or movie, or using graffiti or other unexpected elements to grab people's attention.

Coca-Cola Guerrilla Marketing campaign example:

Coca-Cola campaigns implemented several successful guerrilla marketing campaigns over the years. One example is the "Share a Coke" campaign, which involved printing popular names on Coca-Cola bottles and encouraging people to share the bottles with friends or loved ones whose names were on them.

This campaign was successful because it was a unique and interactive way for Coca-Cola to engage with its customers, and it created a sense of rationalization and exclusivity.

Another example of a guerrilla marketing campaign by Coca-Cola is the "Happiness Machine," which was a vending machine that dispensed unexpected gifts along with the purchased drinks. This campaign was successful because it was a surprise and delight experience for customers, and it generated a lot of buzz and positive word-of-mouth for the brand.

"Coca-Cola Red Discs": In this campaign, Coca-Cola placed red discs with its logo on them in various high-traffic locations, such as sidewalks and bus stops.

These discs were placed in a way that they would only be visible from certain angles, creating a sense of mystery and intrigue for passersby. "Coca-Cola Music": In this campaign, Coca-Cola partnered with music festivals and concerts to create a branded experience for attendees.

This included providing branded merchandise and setting up Coca-Cola-branded areas at the events where attendees could relax and recharge.

"Coca-Cola Happiness Truck": In this campaign, Coca-Cola created a truck that traveled around different cities and dispensed free cans of Coca-Cola to passersby.

This campaign was successful because it created a sense of excitement and surprise for those who encountered the truck, and it generated a lot of buzz and positive word-of-mouth for the brand.

Overall, Coca-Cola's guerrilla marketing campaigns have been successful because they are interactive, unexpected, and create a memorable experience for consumers.

T-Mobile used guerrilla marketing to promote its mobile phone service by creating a series of flash mobs that performed dance routines in public places.

Old Spice - Old Spice used guerrilla marketing to promote its men's grooming products by creating a series of humorous, viral videos featuring actor Isaiah Mustafa.

Samsung - Samsung used guerrilla marketing to promote its Galaxy S3 smartphone by creating a series of "highway billboards" that appeared to be hanging off the side of a bridge, but were actually suspended by wires.

Virgin America - Virgin America used guerrilla marketing to promote its airline by creating a series of "subverting" campaigns, which involved altering existing advertisements in public spaces to promote Virgin America's brand.

Airbnb - Airbnb used guerrilla marketing to promote its home-sharing platform by creating a series of "Night At" events, which allowed people to spend a night in unusual places such as a zoo or a castle, and promoted the idea of unique travel experiences through Airbnb.

IKEA:

IKEA used guerrilla marketing to promote its furniture store by creating a series of "street view" ads that appeared to be real storefronts, but were actually just facades made out of cardboard.

These are just a few more examples of companies that have used guerrilla marketing to promote their products or services in creative and unconventional ways.

overall, Guerrilla marketing could be the answer for your small business. When done correctly, it is often minimal cost while reaching a highly targeted audience. It can also be a terrific way to get noticed, stand out from the crowd, and establish a reputation for being entertaining and unique.

Guerrilla marketing strategies rely heavily on the element of surprise. It aims to produce highly unorthodox campaigns that catch consumers off guard. It is a time investment rather than a financial one. The main investment here is creative and intellectual; its implementation does not have to be costly.

3.PPC Advertising Marketing Strategy:

Pay-per-click (PPC) is an advertising model in which an advertiser pays a fee each time one of their ads is clicked. It's a way of buying visits to your site, rather than attempting to "earn" those visits organically. Search engines like Google and Bing offer PPC advertising through their respective advertising platforms, Google Ads and Bing Ads.
Advertisers bid on keywords that they think their target market will use to search for their products or services, and their ads will appear in the search results when those keywords are used. They only pay when someone clicks on their ad. This can be a cost-effective way of driving traffic to a website, especially if the advertiser only pays when a potential customer clicks on their ad.

In addition to search engines, PPC advertising can also be used on social media platforms like Facebook, Instagram, and LinkedIn, as well as on display networks, which are collections of websites that have agreed to show ads.
When setting up a PPC campaign, advertisers typically choose specific keywords they want to target and set a budget for how much they are willing to spend per click. They also create ad groups, which are collections of ads that target specific keywords. Advertisers can also set geographic and demographic targeting parameters so that their ads are only shown to people in specific locations or age groups.
One of the key benefits of PPC advertising is that it can generate quick results. Unlike organic search engine optimization (SEO), which can take weeks or months to show

results, PPC ads can start generating traffic as soon as they are launched. Additionally, PPC campaigns are highly measurable, so it's easy for advertisers to track how much they are spending, how many clicks their ads are getting, and what their return on investment is.

However, PPC advertising can be costly if not managed effectively. Advertisers must be cautious to keep track of the cost of their campaign and make sure that the cost of the clicks does not exceed the revenue generated from the campaign. Additionally, PPC campaigns require ongoing management and optimization to ensure that they are performing as well as possible.

The first known PPC advertising model was developed in the late 1990s by a company called GoTo.com (later renamed Overture), which was later acquired by Yahoo in 2003. Google also launched its own PPC advertising platform, called AdWords, in 2000.

These early PPC platforms were primarily focused on search advertising, but over time they expanded to include other forms of online advertising, such as display and video advertising. Today, PPC advertising is a major component of digital marketing, with both Google and Facebook operating large and influential PPC advertising platforms.

PPC advertising has become a popular marketing strategy for businesses of all sizes, as it allows them to reach targeted audiences and get their message in front of potential customers at the moment they are searching for products or services like theirs.

The ability to target specific demographics, interests, and behaviors has made PPC advertising a valuable tool for businesses looking to drive sales and increase their online visibility. Additionally, PPC advertising allows businesses to control their advertising costs, as they only pay when someone clicks on their ad.

Over the years, PPC advertising has evolved to become more sophisticated and data-driven. Platforms like Google AdWords and Facebook Ads now use complex algorithms to optimize ad delivery and targeting, making it easier for businesses to get the most out of their advertising spend.

Other innovations, such as remarketing and dynamic ad targeting, have also become popular in recent years, further increasing the effectiveness of PPC advertising.

In summary, Pay-per-click (PPC) advertising is a digital marketing strategy that allows businesses to advertise online and pay only when someone clicks on the ad. This strategy has been around since the late 1990s and has evolved over the years to become more sophisticated and data-driven. Today, it is an essential component of any business' online marketing strategy as it helps to increase online visibility and drive sales.

PPC Advertising Tactics

Some tactics for PPC advertising include:

- Keyword research: Identifying the most relevant and high-performing keywords to target in your PPC campaigns.
- Ad copywriting: Writing compelling ad copy that will entice users to click on your ads.

- Ad targeting: Selecting the right audience to show your ads to by using demographic, geographic, and behavioral targeting options.
- Landing page optimization: Ensuring that the landing page users are directed to after clicking on your ad is optimized for conversions.
- A/B testing: Experimenting with different ad copy, ad targeting options, and landing pages to see which perform the best.
- Bid optimization: Continuously monitoring and adjusting your bid for each keyword to ensure that your ads are shown to the right audience at the right time.
- Campaign tracking and analysis: Using analytics to track the performance of your PPC campaigns and make data-driven decisions to improve them.
- Retargeting: Showing ads to people who have already interacted with your business, website or apps.
- Utilizing ad extensions: Ad extension allows you to add more information to your ads, like a phone number, address, or additional links.
- Ad scheduling: Scheduling your ads to run at specific times of the day or week when your target audience is most likely to be online.
- Negative keyword research: Identifying and excluding keywords that are not relevant to your business or product to avoid wasting ad spend on irrelevant clicks.
- Mobile optimization: Ensuring that your ads and landing pages are optimized for mobile devices, as more and more users access the internet via their smartphones.
- Audience segmentation: Segmenting your audience based on specific characteristics, such as demographics, interests, or behaviors, to create more targeted and effective campaigns.

- Utilizing remarketing: Showing ads to people who have already interacted with your business in the past, such as visiting your website, to encourage them to return and convert.
- Utilizing social media platforms: Utilizing social media platforms such as Facebook, Instagram and LinkedIn to run PPC campaigns and target specific audience.
- Utilizing video ads: Utilizing video ads on platforms like YouTube, Ticktock and Instagram to reach a wider audience and increase brand awareness.
- Utilizing Local PPC: Utilizing local PPC campaigns to target people searching for products or services in a specific geographic area.
- Automation: Utilizing tools and technologies to automate aspects of your PPC campaigns, such as bid management and ad copy optimization, to save time and improve efficiency.

Overall, PPC advertising can be a highly effective way to reach potential customers and drive conversions. However, it's important to continuously monitor and optimize your campaigns to ensure that you are getting the best results possible.

PPC Advertising Marketing Plan:

A pay-per-click (PPC) advertising marketing strategy plan typically includes the following steps:

Define your target audience and create buyer personas.
Research and select relevant keywords for your campaigns.
Set up and optimize your PPC campaigns on platforms such as Google Ads or Bing Ads.
Continuously monitor and analyze campaign performance, making adjustments as necessary.

Use A/B testing to improve ad copy and landing page experience.

Set a budget and track ROI.

Use remarketing techniques to target users who have previously interacted with your website or ads.

Use negative keyword to filter out unwanted click.

Use conversion tracking to measure the effectiveness of your campaigns.

Continuously adapt and optimize your strategy based on the performance data.

Here are a few examples of a PPC advertising marketing strategy plan for different types of businesses:

1. E-commerce store selling outdoor equipment:
Define target audience:
Outdoor enthusiasts, campers, hikers, etc.
Research and select keywords:
"camping gear," "hiking equipment," "backpacking essentials," etc.
Set up campaigns on Google Ads and Bing Ads targeting users searching for these keywords.
Continuously monitor and adjust bid strategies, ad copy, and landing page experience to improve conversion rates.
Use remarketing to target users who have previously viewed outdoor equipment on the website.
Set a budget and track ROI to ensure that the campaigns are profitable.

2. Local service business (e.g. Plumber):
Define target audience:
Homeowners and property managers in the local area.
Research and select keywords: "emergency plumber," "plumbing repair," "drain cleaning," etc.

Set up campaigns on Google Ads and Bing Ads targeting users searching for these keywords in the local area.
Continuously monitor and adjust bid strategies, ad copy, and landing page experience to improve conversion rates.

Use remarketing to target users who have previously searched for a plumber in the local area.
Set a budget and track ROI to ensure that the campaigns are profitable.
3. B2B software company:
Define target audience:
small and medium-sized businesses in a specific industry (e.g. retail, healthcare, etc.).
Research and select keywords: "inventory management software," "point of sale software," "employee scheduling software," etc.
Set up campaigns on Google Ads and Bing Ads targeting users searching for these keywords.
Continuously monitor and adjust bid strategies, ad copy, and landing page experience to improve conversion rates.
Use remarketing to target users who have previously viewed software solutions on the website.
Set a budget and track ROI to ensure that the campaigns are profitable.
Note that the above examples are general and for a specific case a much more detailed plan and research is required.

There was a small e-commerce company that sold handmade crafts and artisanal products. The company had a beautiful website, but they were struggling to drive traffic and generate sales. They knew that they needed to invest in online advertising to reach a wider audience and grow their business.

The company's marketing team began researching different advertising options, and they quickly realized that pay-per-click (PPC) advertising would be the best fit for their business. PPC advertising allows them to reach potential customers who are actively searching for products like theirs, and they only pay when someone clicks on their ad.

The team started with a thorough keyword research to identify the terms and phrases that their target audience was searching for. They used tools like Google Keyword Planner to research high-volume, low-competition keywords that would be most relevant to their products.

They then created a series of ad groups and campaigns within their PPC advertising platform, and they began testing different ad variations to see which ones performed the best. They wrote compelling ad copy, and choose relevant images to accompany their ads. They also set a budget for their PPC advertising campaign and decided on a bid strategy for their keywords. After a few weeks, the company started to see a steady increase in website traffic and sales. They used conversion rate and return on investment (ROI) to measure the success of their PPC advertising campaign. They noticed that certain keywords and ad groups were performing much better than others, and they made adjustments accordingly.

As time passed, the company's PPC advertising marketing strategy plan was refined and became more effective, and their sales increased significantly. The company's website traffic increased, and they were able to reach a wider audience. They also started to generate more leads and sales, which helped them to grow their business.

Many companies use pay-per-click (PPC) advertising as part of their marketing strategy, including e-commerce websites, service providers, and lead generation sites. Some examples of companies that use PPC advertising include Amazon, Google, Bing, Facebook, and Instagram.

Expedia and Booking.com for the travel industry.

LegalZoom and Rocket Lawyer for legal services.

Zillow and Realtor.com for real estate.

Angie's List and HomeAdvisor for home services

LendingTree and Quicken Loans for financial services

Indeed and LinkedIn for job searching

Weight Watchers and Jenny Craig for health and wellness.

E-commerce: Ebay, Etsy, and Wayfair

Retail: Macy's, Target, and Best Buy

Automotive: CarMax, AutoTrader, and Edmunds

Healthcare: WebMD, CVS Health, and United Healthcare

Telecommunications: AT&T, Verizon, and T-Mobile

Technology: Apple, Microsoft, and Dell

Entertainment: Netflix, Disney+, and Spotify

Food and Beverage: Coca-Cola, Pepsi, and McDonald's

Fashion: Nike, Adidas, and Puma.

These are just a few examples, but many other companies across a variety of industries also use PPC advertising to reach potential customers and drive online sales.

PPC Advertising Strategies Types:

There are several types of pay-per-click (PPC) advertising marketing strategies, including:

- Search advertising: This type of PPC advertising appears at the top of search engine results pages (SERPs) when users search for specific keywords.
- Display advertising: This type of PPC advertising appears on websites across the internet and is typically in the form of banner or text ads.
- Social media advertising: This type of PPC advertising appears on social media platforms and can be targeted to specific demographics and interests.
- Shopping advertising: This type of PPC advertising is used to promote specific products on platforms such as Google Shopping.
- Remarketing: This type of PPC advertising targets users who have previously interacted with a business's website or social media account.
- Local Service Ads (LSAs): This type of PPC advertising is for service-based businesses to get their ads appear at the top of Google search results for specific queries.
- Call-only ads: This type of PPC advertising allows customers to call the advertiser directly from the ad, with no need to visit the advertiser's website.
- Video advertising: This type of PPC advertising allows businesses to place ads on video platforms such as YouTube and Vimeo.
- App install ads: This type of PPC advertising is used to promote mobile apps and can be placed on various platforms including social media, search engines, and app stores.

- Dynamic search ads: This type of PPC advertising uses a business's website to generate ads that appear in search results pages, with the headlines and descriptions of the ads automatically generated based on the content of the website.
- Affiliate marketing: This type of PPC advertising involves paying affiliates or other partners to promote a business's products or services.
- Cost-per-action (CPA) advertising: This type of PPC advertising is a pricing model where the advertiser is only charged when a specific action is taken, such as a purchase or a form submission.
- Cost-per-impression (CPI) advertising: This type of PPC advertising is a pricing model where the advertiser is charged based on the number of times the ad is displayed, regardless of whether it is clicked on.
- Cost-per-thousand (CPM) advertising: This type of PPC advertising is a pricing model where the advertiser is charged based on the number of times an ad is viewed.
- Influencer marketing: This type of PPC advertising involves paying influencers to promote a business's products or services on their social media accounts.
- Email marketing: This type of PPC advertising involves sending promotional emails to a business's mailing list.
- Content marketing: This type of PPC advertising involves creating and distributing valuable content to attract and engage an audience with the goal of driving profitable customer action.
- Retargeting: This type of PPC advertising involves showing ads to users who have previously interacted with a business's website or social media account.

- Sponsored content: This type of PPC advertising involves paying for content to be promoted on platforms such as blogs, news sites, or social media.
- Cost-per-engagement (CPE) advertising: This type of PPC advertising is a pricing model where the advertiser is charged based on the number of user interactions with the ad, such as likes, shares, or comments.

It's worth noting that PPC advertising strategies can be combined to create a more effective marketing campaign, depending on the business's goals and target audience.

key benefits of PPC advertising

Pay-per-click (PPC) advertising has several key benefits, including:

Quick results: PPC advertising can drive traffic to a website almost immediately, unlike some other forms of digital marketing which can take longer to have an impact.

Targeted advertising: PPC advertising allows businesses to target specific demographics, interests, and keywords, ensuring that their ads are seen by the right people.

Measurable results: PPC advertising provides detailed data and metrics that allow businesses to track the success of their campaigns and make informed decisions about future advertising efforts.

Flexibility: PPC advertising allows businesses to adjust their campaigns in real-time, making changes to ads, keywords, and budgets as needed.

Cost-effective: PPC advertising is often a cost-effective way for businesses to reach their target audience, especially compared to traditional forms of advertising such as television and radio.

Brand awareness: PPC advertising can help increase brand awareness and visibility among target audience.

Cost-per-action (CPA) pricing: PPC advertising allows businesses to pay only when a specific action is taken, such as a purchase or a form submission, which can help control costs.

Local targeting: PPC advertising allows businesses to target ads to specific geographic locations, which can be useful for businesses with a local customer base.

All in all, Pay-per-click (PPC) advertising is a popular marketing strategy because it allows businesses to target specific audiences and only pay for advertising when a user clicks on their ad. This allows for a more efficient use of advertising dollars, as opposed to traditional forms of advertising where businesses may pay for ad space regardless of whether or not the ad leads to any conversions. Additionally, PPC advertising allows businesses to track the effectiveness of their ads through metrics such as click-through-rate (CTR) and conversion rate, which can help them optimize their campaigns for better performance.

4. Content Marketing Strategy

Content marketing is a strategic marketing approach focused on creating and distributing valuable, relevant, and consistent content to attract and retain a clearly defined audience. The goal is to drive profitable customer action.

Content marketing is not about selling products or services. Instead, it is about creating valuable and informative content that addresses the needs and interests of your target audience. By consistently providing valuable content, you can build trust and credibility with your audience, which can ultimately lead to increased sales.

A content marketing strategy is the plan that guides your content marketing efforts. It outlines the type of content you will create, who you will create it for, and how you will distribute and promote it. A content marketing strategy should be closely aligned with your overall business goals and marketing strategy.

Steps to develop a content marketing strategy:

Define your target audience: Who are you trying to reach with your content?

Set goals for your content marketing: What do you want to achieve with your content?

Research and identify topics: What topics will be most relevant and interesting to your target audience?

Create a content calendar: When will you create and publish your content?

Determine the types of content you will create: What formats will you use to share your content?

Promote your content: How will you get your content in front of your target audience?

Measure and analyze your results: How effective was your content in achieving your goals and reaching your target audience?
Remember, a content marketing strategy is not a one-time effort; it is an ongoing process that requires constant evaluation and adjustment. Align your content with your business goals: Make sure that your content is supporting your overall business goals and objectives.

Focus on creating valuable and engaging content: The key to successful content marketing is to create content that is valuable and interesting to your target audience.
Be consistent: Consistency is important in order to establish trust and credibility with your audience.
Promote your content: In order for your content to be effective, you need to get it in front of the right people. Promote your content through social media, email marketing, and other channels.

Engage with your audience: Encourage your audience to interact with your content by asking questions and providing opportunities for them to share their thoughts and ideas.
Analyze and optimize your content: Use data and analytics to understand what is and isn't working with your content marketing efforts. Use this information to make adjustments and optimize your strategy. Remember, a content marketing strategy is not a set-it-and-forget-it type of plan. It requires ongoing effort and adaptation in order to be effective.

Here are a few more considerations for your content marketing strategy:

Choose the right channels: Think about where your target audience spends their time online and make sure to distribute your content through those channels.

Use visuals: People are more likely to engage with and share content that includes visuals such as images and videos.

Use calls to action: Include calls to action in your content to encourage your audience to take a specific action, such as visiting your website or signing up for your email list.

Collaborate with influences: Consider partnering with influences or industry thought leaders to promote your content and reach a wider audience.

Use A/B testing: Consider using A/B testing to determine which versions of your content are most effective. This can help you optimize your content for better results.

Be patient: Rome wasn't built in a day, and your content marketing strategy won't be either. Be patient and stay the course; results from content marketing often take time to materialize.

Remember, the key to a successful content marketing strategy is to create valuable, relevant, and consistent content that meets the needs of your target audience and helps you achieve your business goals.

Invest in quality: High-quality content is more likely to engage your audience and drive results. Consider investing in professional writers, designers, and other resources to help create the best possible content.

Use data to inform your strategy: Use data and analytics to understand your audience and their preferences, and use this information to guide your content creation and distribution efforts.

Be authentic: Authenticity is key in building trust with your audience. Be transparent and genuine in your content marketing efforts.

Be flexible: Don't be afraid to pivot your strategy if you're not seeing the results you want. Be willing to try new things and make adjustments as needed.

Foster a content-driven culture: Make content a priority within your organization and encourage everyone to get involved in the content creation process.

Remember, a strong content marketing strategy requires a clear understanding of your target audience, a well-defined set of goals, and a commitment to creating and distributing high-quality content. By following these tips, you can develop a successful content marketing strategy that helps you achieve your business objectives.

Content Marketing Tools

There are many tools that can be used for content marketing. Some popular options include:

- Hoot suite: A social media management platform that helps you schedule and publish content, track metrics, and engage with your audience across multiple social media channels.
- Co Schedule: A content marketing and project management tool that allows you to plan, organize, and execute your content marketing strategy.

- Buzz Sumo: A tool that helps you find the most popular content in your industry and analyze what content is performing well with your target audience.
- Ah refs: A comprehensive SEO and content marketing tool that provides data on keyword research, back links, and content performance.
- Canvas: A graphic design tool that makes it easy to create visually appealing images for social media and other marketing materials.
- Grammar: A writing tool that helps you improve the grammar and clarity of your writing, including your marketing content.
- Adobe Creative Cloud: A suite of design and multimedia tools, including Photo shop and Illustrator, that can be used to create high-quality visuals for your content marketing efforts.
- SEMrush: A tool that helps you track your website's performance, research keywords, and analyze your competitors' marketing strategies.
- Moz: A suite of SEO tools that includes keyword research, site audits, and link analysis.
- HubSpot: An all-in-one marketing platform that includes a variety of tools for content creation, SEO, email marketing, and more.
- Mailchimp: An email marketing platform that allows you to create and send newsletters, automated email campaigns, and other marketing emails.
- Google Analytics: A free web analytics service that provides insights into the traffic and behavior of visitors to your website.
- Google Search Console: A free tool that helps you monitor, maintain, and improve your website's presence in Google search results.

- Piktochart: A tool that helps you create infographics, reports, and other visual content to use in your marketing efforts.
- WordPress: A content management system that allows you to create and manage a website or blog, and publish content easily.
- Slideshare: A platform for sharing presentation and visual content, which can be a great way to promote your content and reach a new audience.
- LinkedIn Marketing Solutions: LinkedIn's suite of marketing tools, which includes sponsored content, display ads, and more, can be a valuable way to reach professionals and decision-makers.
- Hootsuite Insights: A social media analytics tool that helps you track the performance of your content on social media and understand your audience better.
- TweetDeck: A Twitter management tool that allows you to schedule tweets, track keywords and hashtags, and engage with your followers.
- MeetEdgar: A social media scheduling tool that helps you recycle and repurpose your old content to keep it fresh and relevant to your audience.
- Content Marketing Plan
- A content marketing plan is a strategy for creating and distributing valuable, relevant, and consistent content to attract and retain a clearly defined audience.
-

It's an ongoing process that involves identifying target audience, creating relevant content, and distributing the content through various channels. The goal of a content marketing plan is to establish trust and credibility with the target audience, and ultimately to drive profitable customer action.

Here are the steps you can follow to create a content marketing plan:

Conduct a content audit: Take stock of the content you already have and identify what's working and what's not.

Develop a content strategy: Decide on the types of content you will create, how you will distribute it, and how you will measure its success.

Create a content calendar: Plan out the specific pieces of content you will create and when you will publish them.

Implement and execute your plan: Create and distribute the content according to your plan.

Evaluate and adjust: Monitor your content marketing efforts and make adjustments as needed to ensure that you are meeting your goals.

Identify your unique value proposition: What sets your content apart from that of your competitors?

Determine your target audience's pain points and needs: What problems are they trying to solve, and how can your content help them?

Consider your distribution channels: How will you reach your target audience with your content? Some options include your company website, social media, email marketing, and paid advertising.

Create a budget and resource plan: Determine how much you can afford to spend on your content marketing efforts and how you will allocate those resources.

Develop a content creation process: Determine who will be responsible for creating the content, how it will be created (e.g. in-house or outsourced), and how it will be reviewed and approved.

Implement tracking and measurement: Use tools like Google Analytics to track the performance of your content and identify areas for improvement.

Remember, a content marketing plan is an ongoing process, so be prepared to continually review and adjust your strategy as needed.

Consistency is key: Consistently creating and distributing high-quality content will help you build trust and credibility with your target audience.

Prioritize quality over quantity: It's better to create a small number of high-quality pieces of content than a large quantity of low-quality content.

Don't forget about SEO: Optimizing your content for search engines can help you reach a wider audience and drive more traffic to your website.

Engage with your audience: Encourage your audience to interact with your content by asking for their comments and feedback.

Utilize different types of content: Mix things up by creating different types of content, such as blog posts, articles, videos, infographics, and more.

Promote your content: Don't just rely on your website or social media followers to see your content. Use paid advertising and outreach to promote your content to new audiences.

Collaborate with influencers and industry experts: Partnering with influencers and industry experts can help you reach a larger audience and add credibility to your content.

Make your content shareable: Encourage your readers to share your content on social media and other platforms. This can help you reach a wider audience and drive more traffic to your website.

Optimize your headlines: Headlines are important because they are the first thing your audience sees and can determine whether or not they will read your content. Make sure your headlines are attention-grabbing, informative, and accurately reflect the content of your piece.

Use visuals: Adding visuals like images and videos to your content can make it more engaging and easier for your audience to understand.

Incorporate calls to action: Encourage your audience to take a specific action after reading your content, such as signing up for your email list or visiting a landing page.

Repurpose your content: Don't be afraid to reuse or repurpose your content in different formats. For example, you could turn a blog post into a video or create an infographic based on your research.

Monitor your competitors: Keep an eye on what your competitors are doing with their content marketing efforts. This can help you stay ahead of the curve and identify opportunities to differentiate yourself.

Make sure your content is valuable and informative: Your audience should be able to take away valuable insights or information from your content.

Use storytelling to engage your audience: People are more likely to remember and connect with stories, so try incorporating storytelling elements into your content.

Personalize your content: Customize your content for different segments of your audience to make it more relevant and engaging.

Experiment with different formats: Don't be afraid to try out new formats, such as podcasts or webinars, to see what works best for your audience.

Utilize social media to promote your content: Social media platforms can be a great way to distribute and promote your content to a wider audience.

Incorporate user-generated content: Encourage your audience to submit their own content, such as reviews or testimonials, to add credibility and authenticity to your brand.

Make sure your content is well-written and error-free: Poorly written or error-filled content can undermine your credibility and turn off your audience.

Keep your content up to date: Make sure your content is current and relevant. This can help you establish yourself as a thought leader in your industry.

Use data and research to support your content: Incorporating data and research can add credibility to your content and help you make a stronger case.

Utilize content upgrades: Offer additional resources, such as ebooks or whitepapers, in exchange for your audience's email addresses. This can help you build your email list and nurture leads.

Consider creating a content hub: A content hub is a central location on your website where you can showcase all of your content in one place. This can make it easier for your audience to find and consume your content.

By following these tips, you can create a comprehensive content marketing plan that helps you effectively reach and engage your target audience.

Here is an example of a content marketing plan for a small business that sells handmade jewelry:

Target audience: Female millennials interested in unique, handmade jewelry.

Goals: Increase website traffic, drive sales, and grow the email list.

Content audit: Conduct a review of the existing content on the company's website and social media channels. Identify what's working well and what could be improved.

Content strategy: Create a mix of blog posts, product reviews, and behind-the-scenes content to give readers a glimpse into the process of creating handmade jewelry.

Share this content on the company's website and social media channels, as well as through targeted email campaigns. Utilize SEO best practices to increase the visibility of the content on search engines.

Content calendar: Plan out a schedule for creating and publishing new content on the company's website and social media channels.

Implementation and execution: Create and publish new content according to the content calendar. Promote the content through social media, email marketing, and paid advertising.

Evaluation and adjustment: Use tools like Google Analytics to track the performance of the content and make adjustments as needed to ensure that it is meeting the goals of the content marketing plan.

Here's an example of how a business might use content marketing management to achieve its goals:

Let's say that a business sells eco-friendly cleaning products and wants to use content marketing to drive sales and increase brand awareness. To do this, they might:

Set goals and objectives: The business might set a goal of increasing website traffic by 50% over the next six months, and a goal of generating at least 100 new leads during that same period.

Define their target audience: The business might identify their target audience as environmentally-conscious consumers who are looking for natural, non-toxic cleaning products. They might create personas to represent different segments of this audience, such as busy working moms and health-conscious retirees.

Create a content calendar: The business might create a content calendar that includes a mix of blog posts, social media posts, and emails that provide valuable information about eco-friendly cleaning products and their benefits. They might schedule this content to be published on a regular basis, such as twice a week for blog posts and daily for social media posts

Produce and promote content: The business might create blog posts that cover topics like "5 Natural Cleaning Products You Can Make at Home" and "The Benefits of Using Eco-Friendly Cleaning Products." They might also create social media posts that share tips and ideas for using their products, and send emails to their email list that promote special offers and discounts.

Measure and analyze results: The business might use tools like Google Analytics and their email marketing platform to track the results of their content marketing efforts. They might measure metrics like website traffic, leads generated, and sales, and use this information to understand what is and isn't working and make adjustments to their strategy as needed.

Make sure your content aligns with your brand: Your content should reflect your brand's values and personality.

Engage with your audience: Respond to comments and questions from your audience to foster a sense of community and build relationships.

Diversify your content distribution channels: Don't rely on just one or two channels to distribute your content. Experiment with different channels to see which ones work best for your business.

Test different types of content: Try creating different types of content, such as blogs, videos, info graphics, and more, to see what resonates best with your audience.

Use data to inform your content marketing strategy: Use data and analytics to understand your audience's preferences and tailor your content accordingly.

By following these tips, you can create a comprehensive content marketing plan that helps you effectively reach and engage your target audience.

5. Social Media Marketing Strategy

A social media marketing strategy is a plan for using social media platforms to achieve marketing goals. It typically includes goals, target audience, and a plan for creating and distributing content, as well as a plan for measuring the success of the marketing efforts.

The goals of a social media marketing strategy can vary depending on the business and its target audience, but some common goals might include increasing brand awareness, generating leads and sales, and engaging with customers.

The target audience for a social media marketing strategy is the group of people that the business is trying to reach and engage with through social media. This audience may be defined by demographics such as age, location, and interests, as well as by their behaviors and activities on social media.

Creating and distributing content is an important part of a social media marketing strategy. This can include creating original content, such as blog posts and videos, or sharing relevant content from other sources. The content should be tailored to the target audience and the goals of the marketing efforts.

Finally, a social media marketing strategy should include a plan for measuring the success of the marketing efforts. This can involve using tools such as social media analytics to track metrics such as engagement, reach, and conversions.

The history of social media marketing can be traced back to the 1970s, when the first forms of social media, such as internet forums, started to appear. However, it wasn't until the late 1990s and early 2000s, with the launch of social networking sites like LinkedIn, MySpace, and eventually Facebook and

Twitter, that social media began to be widely adopted for marketing purposes.

At first, businesses used social media primarily as a way to connect with customers and build brand awareness. As social media platforms became more popular and sophisticated, businesses began to use them for more targeted marketing efforts, such as targeted advertising and content marketing. In the 2010s, the use of social media for marketing became more widespread and sophisticated, with the introduction of new features such as social media analytics and marketing automation tools. In this decade, social media marketing has become an integral part of many businesses' marketing strategies, and it continues to evolve as new social media platforms and marketing techniques emerge.

Social Media Marketing Tools

There are many tools available to help with social media marketing strategy. Here are a few options to consider:

- Hootsuite: This platform allows you to schedule and publish posts, track mentions and engage with your audience, and analyze the performance of your social media campaigns.
- Buffer: This tool helps you schedule and publish posts to multiple social media platforms, as well as track the performance of your campaigns.
- Sprout Social: This platform offers a variety of features, including social media scheduling, team collaboration tools, and advanced analytics to help you optimize your social media strategy.

- BuzzSumo: This tool helps you identify popular content in your industry and track the performance of your own content.
- Canva: This design tool makes it easy to create visually appealing graphics for your social media accounts.
- Later: This platform allows you to schedule Instagram posts and analyze the performance of your content.
- CoSchedule: This tool helps you plan, organize, and promote your content across all of your social media channels.
- SocialBee: This platform offers a range of features including social media scheduling, team collaboration tools, and analytics to help you optimize your social media strategy.
- AgoraPulse: This tool offers features such as social media scheduling, team collaboration, and advanced analytics to help you improve your social media marketing efforts.
- Zoho Social: This platform offers a range of features including social media scheduling, team collaboration tools, and analytics to help you optimize your social media strategy.
- Sendible: This platform offers a range of features including social media scheduling, team collaboration tools, and advanced analytics to help you optimize your social media strategy.
- SocialFlow: This tool uses real-time data to optimize the distribution of your content across your social media channels.
- MavSocial: This platform offers a range of features including social media scheduling, team collaboration tools, and analytics to help you optimize your social media strategy.

- Planable: This tool helps teams collaborate on social media content and preview how it will look on different platforms before publishing.
- EClincher: This platform offers a range of features including social media scheduling, team collaboration tools, and analytics to help you optimize your social media strategy.
- SocialPilot: This platform offers a range of features including social media scheduling, team collaboration tools, and analytics to help you optimize your social media strategy.
- MeetEdgar: This tool allows you to schedule and publish social media content, and also has a feature that recycles your old content to keep your accounts active.
- Later for Business: This platform is specifically designed for businesses and offers features such as social media scheduling, team collaboration tools, and analytics to help you optimize your social media strategy.
- SocialBee: This tool offers a range of features including social media scheduling, team collaboration tools, and analytics to help you optimize your social media strategy.
- Sprinklr: This platform offers a range of features including social media scheduling, team collaboration tools, and analytics to help you optimize your social media strategy.

Keep in mind that different tools may have different features and pricing plans, so it's a good idea to evaluate your needs and do some research to find the best fit for your business. As with the other tools, it's important to consider your specific needs and do some research to find the best fit for your business.

Social Media Marketing Plan

A social media plan is a document that outlines the steps you will take to achieve your social media marketing goals. It should include information about the social media platforms you will use, the types of content you will post, the target audience you are trying to reach, and the frequency of your posts. The plan should also include metrics for tracking your progress and determining the success of your efforts.

Here are some steps you can follow to create a social media plan:

Identify your target audience: Who do you want to reach with your social media marketing efforts? Understanding your target audience will help you determine which social media platforms to use and what types of content to create.

Set marketing goals: What do you want to achieve with your social media marketing efforts? Do you want to increase brand awareness, drive traffic to your website, or generate leads? Setting clear goals will help you measure the success of your social media marketing efforts.

Choose the right social media platforms: Different social media platforms are popular with different demographics, so it's important to choose the platforms that are most likely to reach your target audience.

Develop a content strategy: Determine what types of content you will create and share on social media. Will you create original content or curate content from other sources? Will you focus on text-based posts, visual content, or both?

Engage with your audience: Social media is a two-way conversation, so it's important to engage with your followers. Respond to comments and messages, ask for feedback, and share user-generated content.

Measure and analyze your results: Use tools like Google Analytics and social media analytics to measure the success of your social media marketing efforts. This will help you understand what's working and what's not, and make adjustments to your strategy as needed.

Be consistent: Consistency is key to building a strong presence on social media. Choose a posting schedule and stick to it, and make sure all of your profiles have a cohesive look and feel.

Use hashtags: Hashtags can help you reach a wider audience on social media. Choose relevant hashtags and use them consistently to make it easier for people to find your content.

Collaborate with influencers: Influencer marketing can be a powerful tool for promoting your brand on social media. Consider partnering with influencers in your industry or niche to help reach a larger audience.

Use paid advertising: While organic reach on social media can be limited, paid advertising can help you reach a larger audience. Consider using paid advertising to promote your content or drive traffic to your website.

Engage with industry leaders: Engaging with industry leaders and influencers can help you build relationships and increase your visibility on social media. Share their content, comment on their posts, and participate in industry-specific hashtags to get noticed.

Monitor and adjust your strategy: Social media is always evolving, so it's important to monitor your results and make adjustments to your strategy as needed. Keep an eye on your analytics and be willing to try new things to see what works best for your business.

Use visuals: Visual content, such as images and videos, tends to perform well on social media. Consider using tools like Canva or Adobe Spark to create visually appealing posts.

Use storytelling: Storytelling can be a powerful way to connect with your audience on social media. Share stories about your brand, your customers, or your industry to create a deeper connection with your followers.

Run social media contests: Contests can be a great way to engage your followers and drive traffic to your social media profiles. Consider offering prizes for things like the best user-generated content or the most creative caption for a photo.

Integrate your social media efforts with your overall marketing strategy: Your social media marketing efforts should be integrated with your overall marketing strategy. Make sure that your social media efforts align with your business goals and that they support your other marketing efforts.

Monitor your online reputation: It's important to regularly monitor your online reputation to ensure that you're putting your best foot forward on social media. Use tools like Google Alerts or Mention to stay informed of what people are saying about your brand online.

Seek out partnerships: Partnering with other businesses or organizations can help you reach a larger audience on social media. Consider partnering with complementary businesses or organizations to cross-promote each other's content.

Use polls and surveys: Polls and surveys can be a fun and interactive way to engage your followers on social media. Consider using these tools to gather feedback or gather insights about your target audience.

Use user-generated content: User-generated content, such as reviews and testimonials, can be a powerful form of social proof. Consider encouraging your followers to share their experiences with your brand, and share their content on your social media profiles.

Be responsive: It's important to be responsive on social media, especially when it comes to customer service. Make sure to regularly monitor your social media profiles and respond to comments and messages in a timely manner.

Use social media to showcase your brand's personality: Your social media profiles are an opportunity to show off your brand's personality. Consider using a consistent tone and voice across all of your profiles to create a cohesive brand image.

Try out new features and tools: Social media platforms are constantly adding new features and tools.

Keep an eye on updates and consider experimenting with new features to see how they can benefit your marketing efforts.

Keep up with industry trends: Staying up to date with industry trends can help you stay relevant on social media. Consider following industry-specific hashtags and keeping an eye on industry news to stay informed.

Use analytics and tracking tools: There are a variety of tools available that can help you track the performance of your social media marketing efforts. Make use of these tools to understand what's working and what's not, and adjust your strategy accordingly.

Use A/B testing: A/B testing, also known as split testing, involves creating two versions of a piece of content and testing them to see which performs better. Consider using A/B testing to fine-tune your social media marketing efforts and maximize their effectiveness.

Use automation tools: There are a variety of tools available that can help you automate certain aspects of your social media marketing efforts. For example, you can use a tool to schedule posts in advance, or to automatically share your blog content on your social media profiles.

Use social media to drive traffic to your website: Social media can be a great way to drive traffic to your website. Consider including links to your website in your social media profiles, and use social media to promote your content and drive traffic to your website.

Use social media to gather customer feedback: Social media is a great way to gather customer feedback and insights. Consider using social media to ask your followers for their thoughts and opinions, and use their feedback to improve your products and services.

Be authentic: It's important to be authentic on social media. Don't try to be something you're not, and be transparent about your business and your intentions.

By following a social media plan, you can effectively use social media to achieve your marketing goals and build a strong online presence.

Here is an example of a social media plan for a small business:
Goals:
Increase brand awareness among our target audience.
Generate leads through social media by directing traffic to our website.
Target audience:
Small business owners in the local area
Ages 25-45.
Interested in improving their marketing efforts.
Platforms:

Facebook
Instagram
LinkedIn

Content calendar:
Monday: Share a blog post from our website
Wednesday: Share a tip or piece of advice related to marketing
Friday: Share a customer testimonial or success story.

Frequency:
3 posts per week.
Engagement:
Respond to comments and messages within 24 hours
Share user-generated content when appropriate
Run polls and ask for feedback from followers.
Measurement:
Track website traffic from social media sources using Google Analytics
Use social media management software to track engagement and follower growth.
Another example of a social media plan for a non-profit organization:

Goals:
Raise awareness about our cause
Encourage followers to take action (e.g., donate, volunteer).
Target audience:
Individuals who are interested in social and environmental issues
Ages 18-34
Located in the United States.

Platforms:
Twitter
Instagram
Facebook

Content calendar:
Monday: Share a quote related to our cause
Tuesday: Share an article or news story about an issue we are addressing
Thursday: Share a personal story from one of our beneficiaries
Friday: Share a call to action (e.g., "Donate now to help us make a difference").

Frequency:
4 posts per week.
Engagement:
Respond to comments and messages within 48 hours
Use hashtags related to our cause to reach a wider audience
Use Instagram Stories to share behind-the-scenes content and highlight the work we are doing.

Measurement:
Track website traffic from social media sources using Google Analytics
Use social media management software to track engagement and follower growth
Track donations and volunteers through our database.
Another example of a social media plan for an e-commerce business:

Goals:
Increase sales through social media by directing traffic to our website

Build brand loyalty and increase customer retention.
Target audience:
Individuals interested in fashion and accessories
Ages 18-34
Located in the United States.

Platforms:
Instagram.
Piterest.
Facebook.

Content calendar:
Monday: Share a product from our store
Wednesday: Share a customer photo or review
Friday: Share a behind-the-scenes look at our company or team.

Frequency:
3 posts per week.
Engagement:
Respond to comments and messages within 24 hours
Share user-generated content when appropriate
Run Instagram and Facebook ads targeting our target audience.

Measurement:
Track website traffic from social media sources using Google Analytics
Use social media management software to track engagement and follower growth
Track sales and customer retention through our e-commerce platform.

By following this plan, the e-commerce business can increase its sales, build brand loyalty, and engage with its target audience through social media.

Companies Use Social Media

Many companies use social media marketing strategies to reach and engage with their target audience. Some examples of companies that use social media marketing include:

Amazon

Apple

Coca-Cola

Disney

eBay

Facebook

Google

Instagram

Nike

Starbucks

Amazon:

Amazon uses social media marketing strategies as a way to reach and engage with its customers.

Amazon has a strong presence on several social media platforms, including Facebook, Twitter, Instagram, and YouTube, and uses these platforms to promote its products, offers, and services. Amazon also uses social media to provide customer support and respond to customer inquiries and concerns.

In addition to its own social media accounts, Amazon also encourages its customers to share their experiences with its products on social media and to use specific hashtags when doing so. This helps to create a sense of community and encourage customer engagement with the brand.

Apple:Apple does use social media marketing strategies. Apple has a presence on many social media platforms, including Facebook, Twitter, Instagram, LinkedIn, and YouTube.

The company uses these platforms to promote its products and services, engage with customers, and share company news and updates.

Apple also uses social media to run promotional campaigns and contests, and to share content such as videos, articles, and blog posts.

This is just a small sample of the many companies that use social media marketing. Many small businesses and startups also use social media as part of their marketing efforts.

Here's a story about a small business owner who used social media marketing to grow their business:

Samantha was a jewelry designer who had always dreamed of turning her passion into a successful business.

She started by selling her pieces at local craft fairs and markets, but she knew that she needed to reach a larger audience to truly grow her business. That's when she decided to try social media marketing.At first, Samantha was overwhelmed by the number of different social media platforms and wasn't sure where to start. She decided to focus on Instagram, since it seemed to be the most popular platform for artists and small businesses. She spent some time researching hashtags and learning about the best times to post.

Samantha began posting pictures of her latest pieces and offering special discounts to her followers. She also engaged with other users by commenting on their posts and responding to their comments on her own content. Over time, her following grew and she started to receive orders from people all over the country.

Samantha was thrilled by the success of her social media marketing efforts and decided to expand her reach by also using Facebook and Pinterest.

She continued to post engaging content and interact with her followers, and her business continued to grow.

Within a few months, Samantha had gone from selling her pieces at local markets to shipping orders all over the world. She was grateful for the power of social media marketing and knew that it had played a crucial role in the success of her business.Finally As part of a social media marketing strategy, you can employ a variety of strategies. Among the alternatives are:

Determine which social media platforms your target audience is using and focus your efforts there.

Develop a content calendar to help plan and organize your posts.

Use visuals and graphics to help make your content more engaging.

Utilize hashtags to make your content more discover able.

Engage with your followers by responding to comments and messages.

Run social media ads targeted at your desired audience.

Collaborate with influencers or other businesses to reach a wider audience.

Use analytics tools to track the performance of your posts and understand what works best.

Consider using automation tools to help manage and schedule your social media activity.

Remember to also consider your overall business goals and the specific goals you have for your social media efforts. This will help guide your strategy and ensure that your tactics are aligned with your objectives.

6. Email marketing strategy

Email marketing is a strategy that involves sending promotional or informative messages to a target audience via email. The goal of email marketing is typically to build brand awareness, establish trust, generate leads, or encourage conversions, such as making a purchase or signing up for a service.

Email marketing is a form of direct marketing that uses electronic mail as a means of communicating commercial or fundraising messages to an audience. In its broadest sense, every email sent to a potential or current customer could be considered email marketing. However, the term is usually used to refer to:

Sending emails with the purpose of enhancing the relationship of a merchant with its current or old customers, to encourage customer loyalty and repeat business.

Sending emails with the purpose of acquiring new customers or convincing current customers to purchase something immediately. Adding advertisements to emails sent by other companies to their customers.

Email marketing has been around since the 1970 s, but it has evolved significantly over the years. In the early days, emails were primarily used to send text-based messages, but today they can include images, videos, and other interactive elements. Email marketing campaigns can be highly targeted and personalized, making them an effective way for businesses to reach their customers.

There are several steps involved in creating an email marketing campaign:

Define your target audience: Who do you want to send your emails to?

Create a list of email addresses: How will you collect email addresses from your target audience?

Design your emails: What will your emails look like? Will they include images, videos, or other media?

Write compelling content: What message do you want to convey through your emails? How will you engage your audience and encourage them to take action?

Set up an email marketing platform: How will you send your emails and track their performance?

Test and optimize: How will you test different versions of your emails to see which ones perform the best?

Analyze and report on results: How will you track the success of your email marketing campaign and use that information to improve future campaigns?

Here are a few additional points to consider as part of your email marketing strategy

Segmentation: One effective way to improve the effectiveness of your email marketing is to segment your email list into smaller groups based on common characteristics, such as location, interests, or past behavior.

This allows you to tailor your messaging and offers to each group, making them more relevant and engaging.

Professionalization: You can also use Professionalization techniques, such as using the recipient's name in the subject line or body of the email, to make your messages feel more relevant and personalized to the individual.

A/B testing: It can be helpful to conduct A/B tests, where you send two slightly different versions of the same email to a small group of recipients and see which one performs better.

This can help you identify which elements of your emails are most effective and make data-driven improvements.

Automation: Email marketing platforms often allow you to set up automated email campaigns that are triggered by certain actions, such as when a user signs up for your email list or makes a purchase.

This can help you save time and ensure that your emails are being sent to the right people at the right time.

Mobile optimization: With more and more people accessing emails on their mobile devices, it's important to make sure your emails are optimized for mobile viewing. This includes using a responsive design and keeping the email concise and to the point.

Legal considerations: There are also a number of legal considerations to keep in mind when sending marketing emails, such as the CAN-SPAM Act in the US and the General Data Protection Regulation (GDPR) in the EU.

It's important to familiarize yourself with these regulations and ensure that you are following them when sending marketing emails.

Use a clear and concise subject line: The subject line is often the first thing that a recipient sees, and it's important to make it interesting and informative enough to entice them to open the email.

Keep it short and to the point, and avoid using spammy or misleading language.

Make the most of your preheader text: The preheader text is the snippet of text that appears next to or below the subject line in the email inbox. This is a great opportunity to give recipients a sense of what's in the email and encourage them to open it.

Keep your emails brief and focused: No one wants to read a long, rambling email, so it's important to keep your messages concise and to the point. Focus on one or two main points and use bullet points or numbered lists to make the information easy to scan.

Use images and other media sparingly: While images and videos can be a great way to make your emails more engaging, it's important to use them sparingly and ensure that they add value to the email. Large, unoptimized images can slow down the loading time of your emails and turn off recipients.

Make it easy for recipients to take action: Your emails should have a clear call to action (CTA) that tells recipients what you want them to do next, whether it's signing up for a service, making a purchase, or visiting your website. Make sure your CTA is prominent and easy to see.

Use Alt tags for images: If an email client doesn't display images by default, it will display the Alt tag text instead. This is a great opportunity to include additional information or a call to action in your emails.

Include social media links: Encourage recipients to connect with you on social media by including links to your social media profiles in your emails. This can help you build awider audience and increase engagement with your brand.

Email Marketing Strategy Tools:

There are several tools available that can help you with your email marketing strategy. Here are a few options:

Mailchimp:
This is a popular email marketing platform that offers a range of features, including email templates, automation, and analytics.

Constant Contact:
This is another email marketing tool that offers templates, automation, and analytics, as well as integrations with social media and e-commerce platforms.

HubSpot:
This is a comprehensive marketing platform that includes email marketing features, along with tools for social media, SEO, and content management.
ActiveCampaign:
This is an email marketing tool that offers automation, personalization, and integrations with CRM and e-commerce platforms.

GetResponse:
This is an email marketing platform that offers a range of templates, automation, and analytics, as well as integrations with social media and webinar platforms.

Sendinblue:
This is an email marketing platform that offers a range of features, including templates, automation, and analytics, as well as SMS and chat capabilities.

AWeber:
This is an email marketing tool that offers templates, automation, and analytics, as well as integrations with social media and e-commerce platforms.

Klaviyo:
This is an email marketing platform that is designed specifically for e-commerce businesses, and offers features such as automation, personalization, and integrations with popular e-commerce platforms.

Campaign Monitor:
This is an email marketing platform that offers a range of templates, automation, and analytics, as well as integrations with CRM and social media platforms.

Omnisend:
This is an email marketing platform designed specifically for e-commerce businesses, and offers features such as automation, personalization, and integrations with popular e-commerce platforms.

MailerLite:
This is an email marketing platform that offers a range of features, including templates, automation, and analytics, as well as integrations with social media and e-commerce platforms.

iContact:
This is an email marketing tool that offers templates, automation, and analytics, as well as integrations with social media and CRM platforms.

Drip:
This is an email marketing platform that is designed specifically for e-commerce businesses, and offers features such as automation, personalization, and integrations with popular e-commerce platforms.

MailJet:
This is an email marketing platform that offers a range of features, including templates, automation, and analytics, as well as integrations with CRM and e-commerce platforms.

ConvertKit:
This is an email marketing tool that is designed specifically for bloggers and content creators, and offers features such as automation, opt-in forms, and integrations with popular blogging platforms.

VerticalResponse:
This is an email marketing platform that offers a range of features, including templates, automation, and analytics, as well as integrations with social media and e-commerce platforms.

Mad Mimi:
This is an email marketing tool that offers templates, automation, and analytics, as well as integrations with social media and e-commerce platforms.

Campaigner:
This is an email marketing platform that offers a range of features, including templates, automation, and analytics, as well as integrations with CRM and e-commerce platforms.

ExactTarget:
This is an email marketing platform that offers a range of features, including templates, automation, and analytics, as well as integrations with CRM and e-commerce platforms.

StreamSend:
This is an email marketing tool that offers a range of features, including templates, automation, and analytics, as well as integrations with social media and e-commerce platforms.

Bronto:
This is an email marketing platform that offers a range of features, including templates, automation, and analytics, as well as integrations with CRM and e-commerce platforms.

Pardot:
This is an email marketing tool that is part of the Salesforce Marketing Cloud, and offers features such as automation, personalization, and integrations with CRM and e-commerce platforms.

Marketo:
This is an email marketing platform that offers a range of features, including templates, automation, and analytics, as well as integrations with CRM and e-commerce platforms.

Infusionsoft:
This is an email marketing tool that offers a range of features, including templates, automation, and analytics, as well as integrations with CRM and e-commerce platforms.

Emma:

This is an email marketing platform that offers a range of features, including templates, automation, and analytics, as well as integrations with social media and e-commerce platforms.

It's worth considering the specific needs of your business when selecting an email marketing tool. You may want to compare features, pricing, and reviews before making a decision.

Email Marketing Strategy Plan:

An email marketing strategy is a plan for using email to reach and engage with your target audience, and to promote and sell your products or services. Here are some steps you can follow to create a successful email marketing strategy:

Define your goals: What do you want to achieve with your email marketing? Do you want to drive sales, generate leads, or keep your customers informed and engaged? Clearly defining your goals will help you create a strategy that is tailored to your needs.

Identify your target audience: Who are you trying to reach with your emails? Understanding your target audience will help you create messages that resonate with them and encourage them to take action.

Segment your email list: Segmenting your email list allows you to send targeted and personalized messages to different groups of subscribers. For example, you might segment your list by demographic information, location, or interests.

Choose an email marketing platform: There are many different email marketing platforms available, each with its own set of features and capabilities. Choose a platform that meets your needs and budget.

Create a content calendar: A content calendar helps you plan and schedule your emails in advance. This can include newsletters, promotional emails, abandoned cart emails, and other types of messages.

Test, optimize, and analyze: Test different subject lines, email designs, and call-to-action buttons to see what works best. Use analytics tools to track the performance of your emails and identify areas for improvement. By following these steps, you can create a comprehensive email marketing strategy that helps you achieve your business goals and connect with your audience.

Here is an example of an email marketing strategy for a small e-commerce business:

Goals:
Increase sales and customer engagement.
Target audience:
Women aged 25-45 who are interested in fashion and beauty.
Segmentation:
Segment email list by location (US, Canada, Europe) and purchase history (first-time buyers, repeat customers).
Email marketing platform:
Mailchimp.
Content calendar:
Monday: Newsletter with featured. products, styling tips, and special promotions.
Wednesday: Abandoned cart email for items left in customers' shopping carts.
Friday: Promotional email with special deals and discounts.
Testing and optimization:

Test different subject lines to see which ones have the highest open rates.

Experiment with different email designs to see which ones have the highest click-through rates.

Use A/B testing to compare the performance of different call-to-action buttons.

Analysis:

Use Mailchimp's analytics tools to track the performance of each email and identify trends and patterns. Use this information to inform future campaigns and make data-driven decisions.

Here is another example of an email marketing strategy for a B2B software company:

Goals:

Generate leads and nurture leads through the sales funnel.

Target audience:

Small to medium-sized businesses in the tech industry.

Segmentation:

Segment email list by company size and industry.

Email marketing platform:

Constant Contact.

Content calendar:

Monday: Welcome email for new subscribers with a special offer

Wednesday: Educational email with a blog post or white paper on a relevant topic

Friday: Case study or testimonial email highlighting the success of a current customer.

Testing and optimization:

Test different subject lines to see which ones have the highest open rates.

Experiment with different email designs to see which ones have the highest click-through rates.

Use A/B testing to compare the performance of different call-to-action buttons.

Analysis:

Use Constant Contact's analytics tools to track the performance of each email and identify trends and patterns. Use this information to inform future campaigns and make data-driven decisions.

Here is another example of an email marketing strategy for a non-profit organization:

Goals: Increase donations and engagement with volunteers.

Target audience: Potential donors and volunteers in the local community.

Segmentation: Segment email list by location and past donation history.

Email marketing platform: Campaign Monitor.

Content calendar:

Monday: Newsletter with updates on current and upcoming events.

Wednesday: Personalized email thanking a donor for their past support and asking for a recurring donation.

Friday: Volunteer spotlight email featuring a current volunteer and their experiences with the organization.

Testing and optimization:

Test different subject lines to see which ones have the highest open rates.

Experiment with different email designs to see which ones have the highest click-through rates.

Use A/B testing to compare the performance of different call-to-action buttons.

Analysis: Use Campaign Monitor's analytics tools to track the performance of each email and identify trends and patterns. Use this information to inform future campaigns and make data-driven decisions.

Email Marketing Companies

Email marketing is a popular marketing strategy used by many companies of all sizes. Some examples of well-known companies that use email marketing include Amazon, eBay, and Groupon.

These companies often send promotional emails to their customers to advertise sales, new products, and other special offers. Many smaller businesses and startups also use email marketing as a way to reach their target audience and promote their products or services.

Here is an example of an email marketing strategy that a company like Amazon might use:

Define the target audience: Amazon would likely segment their email list based on customer demographics, purchase history, and other data points.

Set goals: Amazon's goals for their email marketing campaigns might include driving sales, increasing brand awareness, or promoting a new product or service.

Develop a content calendar: Amazon would create a schedule for sending out emails, including newsletters, promotional offers, and other types of content.

Create email campaigns: Amazon would design and write the emails, using engaging subject lines, personalized messaging, and eye-catching graphics to encourage readers to take action.

Test and optimize: Amazon would use A/B testing to determine the best time to send emails, the most effective subject lines, and other variables that could impact the success of their campaigns.

Analyze and report: Amazon would track the performance of their email campaigns and use the data to identify areas for improvement and to inform future strategies.

Overall, the goal of Amazon's email marketing strategy would be to build customer loyalty and drive revenue through targeted, personalized communications.

Here is an example of an email marketing strategy that a company like eBay might use:

Define the target audience: eBay would segment their email list based on customer demographics, purchase history, and other data points to ensure that they are targeting the right people with their campaigns.

Set goals: eBay's goals for their email marketing campaigns might include driving traffic to the site, promoting new products or sales, or increasing customer engagement.

Develop a content calendar: eBay would create a schedule for sending out emails, including newsletters, promotional offers, and other types of content.

Create email campaigns: eBay would design and write the emails, using engaging subject lines, personalized messaging, and eye-catching graphics to encourage readers to take action.

Test and optimize: eBay would use A/B testing to determine the best time to send emails, the most effective subject lines, and other variables that could impact the success of their campaigns.

Analyze and report: eBay would track the performance of their email campaigns and use the data to identify areas for improvement and to inform future strategies.

Overall, the goal of eBay's email marketing strategy would be to increase customer engagement and drive sales through targeted, personalized communications.

Email Marketing Strategy Types:

There are several types of email marketing strategies that businesses and organizations can use to reach their target audience and achieve their marketing goals. Some common types of email marketing strategies include:

1. Email Marketing Strategy Newsletters:
An email marketing newsletter is a type of email that is sent to a list of subscribers who have opted in to receive updates from a business.

Newsletters can be used to inform subscribers about new products, sales, or other events, or to provide educational or helpful information related to the business's industry.

Here are a few tips for creating an effective email marketing newsletter:

Keep it focused: Don't try to cover too many different topics in one newsletter. Instead, choose one main theme and stick to it.

Personalize the content: Use the subscriber's name in the subject line and throughout the email to make it feel more personalized.

Make it visually appealing: Use images, videos, and other multimedia elements to make the newsletter more engaging.

Keep it short and sweet: No one wants to read a long, rambling email. Keep your newsletter concise and to the point.
Segment your list: Not all subscribers are interested in the same things. Use list segmentation to send targeted newsletters to different groups of subscribers based on their interests.

2. **Email Marketing Strategy Drip campaigns:**

A drip campaign is a type of email marketing strategy that involves sending a series of automated emails to a list of subscribers over a period of time.
Drip campaigns are often used to nurture leads and guide them through the sales funnel by providing them with relevant information and offers at each stage of the buying process.

Here are a few tips for creating an effective drip campaign:

Define your goals: What do you want to achieve with your drip campaign? Do you want to generate leads, convert leads into customers, or upsell to existing customers
Segment your list: Not all subscribers are at the same stage in the buying process. Use list segmentation to send targeted emails to different groups of subscribers based on their interests and actions.
Create a schedule: Determine how often you want to send emails and what the content of each email will be.
Use trigger events: Set up your drip campaign to send emails based on specific actions that subscribers take, such as visiting a particular page on your website or clicking a link in an email.

Monitor and analyze: Use email marketing software to track the performance of your drip campaign and make adjustments as needed.

3. Email Marketing Strategy Targeted emails:
Targeted emails are emails that are sent to specific individuals or groups of people based on their interests or actions. This type of email marketing strategy can be very effective because it allows you to send personalized and relevant messages to your subscribers.

Here are a few tips for creating targeted emails:

Segment your list: Use list segmentation to divide your email list into smaller groups based on factors such as location, interests, or actions taken.
Personalize the content: Use the subscriber's name in the subject line and throughout the email to make it feel more personalized.
Use trigger events: Set up your email marketing software to send targeted emails based on specific actions that subscribers take, such as visiting a particular page on your website or clicking a link in an email.
Test and optimize: Use A/B testing to try out different subject lines, headlines, and other elements of the emails to see what works best for each segment of your list.
Monitor and analyze: Use email marketing software to track the performance of your targeted emails and make adjustments as needed.

4. Email Marketing Strategy Transactional emails

Transactional emails are automated emails that are sent to customers in response to a specific action or event, such as making a purchase or signing up for a service.
These emails are typically triggered by a transaction or interaction with a business and are not part of a regular email marketing campaign.

Here are a few tips for creating effective transactional emails:

Make the subject line clear and relevant: The subject line should clearly communicate the purpose of the email and the action that the customer took that triggered it.
Personalize the content: Use the customer's name in the email and any other relevant information, such as their order number or account details.
Keep it concise: Transactional emails should only include the information that is necessary for the customer to complete the transaction or understand the event that triggered the email.
Use a clear and simple design: Transactional emails should be easy to read and navigate, with a clear call to action.
Monitor and analyze: Use email marketing software to track the performance of your transactional emails and make adjustments as needed.

5. Email Marketing Strategy Referral emails:
Referral emails are emails that are sent to customers or clients to encourage them to refer their friends, family, or colleagues to your business. This type of email marketing strategy can be an effective way to generate new leads and drive sales.

Here are a few tips for creating effective referral emails:
Make it easy for customers to refer others: Provide a simple and clear call to action in the email, such as a referral link or a coupon code that the referred person can use.
Personalize the content: Use the customer's name in the email and any other relevant information, such as the products or services they have purchased from you.
Offer an incentive: Consider offering a reward or discount to customers who refer others to your business. This can increase the chances that they will actually make the referral.
Use social proof: Include testimonials or case studies from satisfied customers in the email to demonstrate the value of your products or services.

Test and optimize: Use A/B testing to try out different subject lines, headlines, and other elements of the email to see what works best.
Monitor and analyze: Use email marketing software to track the performance of your referral emails and make adjustments as needed.
6. Email Marketing Strategy Event invitations:
Event invitations are emails that are sent to invite people to attend a specific event, such as a webinar, seminar, or workshop. This type of email marketing strategy can be an effective way to promote an event and generate interest in it.

Here are a few tips for creating effective event invitations:

Make the subject line compelling: The subject line should be attention-grabbing and clearly convey the purpose of the event.
Provide all the necessary information: The invitation should include details such as the date, time, location, and any other relevant information about the event.

Use images and graphics: Use images and graphics to make the invitation more visually appealing and to better convey the theme or purpose of the event.

Use a clear and simple design: The invitation should be easy to read and navigate, with a clear call to action.

Use social proof: Include testimonials or case studies from satisfied attendees of previous events in the email to build excitement and credibility.

Test and optimize: Use A/B testing to try out different subject lines, headlines, and other elements of the email to see what works best.

Monitor and analyze: Use email marketing software to track the performance of your event invitations and make adjustments as needed.

7. Email Marketing Strategy Re-engagement emails:
Re-engagement emails are emails that are sent to inactive or unengaged subscribers in an effort to get them to re-engage with your business.

This type of email marketing strategy can be used to prevent subscribers from opting out of your email list or to encourage them to make a purchase or take some other desired action.

Here are a few tips for creating effective re-engagement emails:

Make the subject line compelling: The subject line should be attention-grabbing and clearly convey the purpose of the email. Personalize the content: Use the subscriber's name in the email and any other relevant information, such as their past purchases or interests.

Offer an incentive: Consider offering a discount or other special offer to encourage inactive subscribers to re-engage with your business.

Use a clear and simple design: The email should be easy to read and navigate, with a clear call to action.

Overall, Email marketing is popular because it is an effective way to reach a large audience at a relatively low cost. When done correctly, email marketing can be an effective way to build relationships with customers and prospects, nurture leads, and drive sales. Additionally, email marketing can be easily tracked and measured, so you can see how well your campaigns are performing and make adjustments as needed. Finally, email is a familiar and convenient medium for many people, so they are more likely to engage with marketing messages that are delivered via email.

Meet Samir Saif

Samir Saif, a legal advisor and entrepreneur from Egypt with a wealth of experience in the establishment of companies and startups in the fields of programming, technology, and business management. Samir specializes in seamlessly integrating the legal aspect with programming matters, making it easier for entrepreneurs to launch and grow their businesses.

Throughout Samir's career, Samir has worked closely with a wide range of clients, from early-stage startups to established companies, to help them navigate the complex legal landscape of the tech industry.

Samir Saif has a deep understanding of the specific challenges and opportunities that come with starting and growing a tech-based business, and uses this knowledge to provide tailored, strategic advice to clients.

In addition to Samir's legal expertise, Samir Saif is also well-versed in the latest trends and developments in the tech industry, allowing Samir Saif to not only provide legal guidance, but also identify potential opportunities and help clients stay ahead of the curve.

As a successful entrepreneur, Samir Saif understands the importance of taking a hands-on approach and working closely with clients to help them achieve their goals. Whether it's incorporating a new business, negotiating contracts, or protecting intellectual property, Samir Saif is dedicated to helping clients succeed.

Samir believes that by combining legal expertise with an understanding of the tech industry, Samir can play a crucial role in the success of the companies and startups Samir Saif works with. Samir Saif looks forward to continuing to help them achieve their goals and reach their potential in the future.